The Complete Guide to Owning and Operating a Home-Based Recruiting Business

The Complete Guide to Owning and Operating a Home-Based Recruiting Business

A Step-by-Step Business Plan for Entrepreneurs

Charrissa D. Cawley

Writers Club Press
San Jose New York Lincoln Shanghai

The Complete Guide to Owning and Operating
a Home-Based Recruiting Business
A Step-by-Step Business Plan for Entrepreneurs

Writers Club Press
an imprint of iUniverse.com, Inc.

For information address:
iUniverse.com, Inc.
5220 S 16th, Ste. 200
Lincoln, NE 68512
www.iuniverse.com

This publication provides the author's opinion with regard to the subject
matter contained herein. Neither the publisher or the author intends, with this
publication, to render accounting, legal or any other professional advice. The
publisher and author disclaim any personal liability, risk or loss incurred as a
consequence of the use and application, either directly or indirectly, of any
advice, methods or information presented herein.

ISBN: 0-595-16395-5

Printed in the United States of America

It is with gratitude that
I dedicate this book to my husband, Jeff,
for believing in me and supporting me
in every endeavor I undertake.

Contents

Acknowledgements

I would like to thank the following people:

My editor Bob Drews, a brilliant man, whom I hold the highest regard for

My publishing services associates, Joyce Greenfield & Dan Sylvia

My mother, father, brother, sisters and grandparents for their unconditional love and support

My wonderful husband Jeffrey, who never let me lose sight of why I set out to conquer this project

Introduction

How to Think Like an Entrepreneur

There is a popular misconception about entrepreneurs these days. Supposedly, entrepreneurs are strong-willed people of action. However, the truth is that successful entrepreneurs are strong-willed men and women, first of thought and then of action. Every single day, the primary action is thinking and relentlessly seeking more information to enable them to continually give their clients what they need.

Having information and knowing how to utilize it is the key to business strength. Information is the great equalizer. It has no bias toward gender, religion or race. In its simplest form, information is a single fact. It is indeed anything that you see, hear, touch, talk about, observe or question. Information is the raw material for your thinking. It is anything that enters your mind. A constant flow of new information is the only way to keep a pulse on your business. Anticipate and prepare for your future and set your priorities straight.

You use bits and pieces of information to make key decisions and then take action every day. No matter what industry you choose to be involved in, the absolute key to your success will be how well you can handle information in the three main areas of your business: Marketing, Management and Money. These tools are like three legs on a stool. You cannot sit on the stool if one of the legs is broken or missing. It is imperative that you understand what information is, what information you need in your business, where to get it and how to use it.

There is nothing more important in business. You will need all of the information about every aspect of your business from day one if you plan to get off to a strong start. If you are going into business for yourself for the very first time, prepare to go through a kind of human revolution as you develop your skills, methods and experience at gathering information. You need to sort, question, analyze, dissect, interpret, reflect on and organize.

You will be dealing with a more comprehensive scope of information than ever before. Eventually it will come naturally, like brushing your teeth in the morning. The better and faster you get at thinking about and gathering information, the more natural it will become. It is exercise for the mind and it is for your own benefit that you learn to love it!

Chapter One

Getting Started

It is estimated that 2,000,000 businesses are started each year. However, many of those businesses do not survive in their original form. They may merge with other ventures, alter their business strategies or simply fail. Whether you are operating a recruiting business or selling pencils, you must take the time to think through your strategies and recognize your own strengths and limitations.

Starting your own business requires a large investment of time and while the thought of operating a home-based business may seem very attractive, it isn't for everyone. There are substantial risks. To have even a chance of success, you must set yourself apart from your competition. Educate yourself on the industry and the market space you plan to enter. Your clients are now your bosses. You will need to keep up with what's going on in your industry. It is important for you to have a focus from day one. Learn who your competitors are, take a management course, identify the markets you plan to serve, attend seminars and conferences that pertain to those markets and make sure that your lifestyle will allow you to meet the demands of business ownership. Examine both your strengths and weaknesses before you begin so that you will have the opportunity to remedy the factors that may impede your success further down the line. The following is a list of both advantages and disadvantages of working out of your home:

Advantages:

The key advantage to working out of your home is that you can set your own schedule and hours. You can begin each day at whatever time you please, you can take as many breaks as you see necessary, and you can take a two hour lunch as opposed to a half hour if you choose to do so.

You are your own boss. There is great satisfaction in knowing that you don't have a supervisor breathing down your neck. It's also nice to be able to avoid the constant interruptions you sometimes get when working in a corporate atmosphere.

You control your income. There is no ceiling on the amount of money you can make if your business is a success. Your income is a direct result of the time and effort you invest in your business.

You don't have to hassle with a daily commute. Owning your own home-based business also allows for more time with your family and friends, which is a rare commodity these days for those out there in Corporate America.

Disadvantages:

Although there are several wonderful advantages to working out of your home, you should always consider the following:

If you are not a motivated, self-starter type who can keep to a set schedule and manage your time efficiently, you may want to think things through very carefully before starting your own business.

You may not be able to handle all of the distractions from the television, the kids, the telephone and other demands.

You may feel isolated from your colleagues or peers.

You have no source of guaranteed income as with a salaried position and may encounter dry spells of little or no income.

Some Helpful Tips:

Set aside a separate room in your home or apartment for your business. Set a definite work schedule and try to stick to it as much as possible. Have a separate phone line with an answering system for your business. Get out of the house at least once a day just as you normally would get out for lunch each day in the office.
Keep in touch with your friends as well as former colleagues and peers.

Financial benefits from having an office at home:

In 1986 a law called the Tax Reform Act was passed. This law made some very important changes in home office deductions. Besides all of your normal business deductions, here are a few special deductions that you may be able to benefit from:
As long as you are using a portion of your home or apartment exclusively and regularly for business purposes, you can sometimes deduct a portion of your expenses. Consult your accountant or tax adviser for what constitutes "exclusive" or "regularly."
You may have deductions that qualify under regular business expenses and are necessary for the operation of your business but are not included in the home office deductions. (telephone bills, travel, etc.)
Each person's situation is very different. You may be able to deduct many other things such as rent and electricity. Once again, you must consult with your accountant or tax adviser for details.

Tax Responsibilities:

Since you work out of your home, you are considered to be self-employed. Therefore, you no longer have an employer deducting taxes out of your check each week. You will be held responsible for claiming and paying your own income taxes. These payments will include federal self-employment tax/Social Security. If and when you ever decided to hire employees, there are separate responsibilities that need to be discussed with an accountant or tax adviser.

Insurance:

You can get insurance from your insurance agent that extends the normal coverage under your homeowner's policy or apartment dweller's policy for any business guest you may have. You may decide to take out a business property insurance policy for your business equipment such as your fax machine, computer and any other office equipment. These types of insurance we have described are not mandatory or necessary to run your business. They are all optional.

Legal Questions:

Is a business license required to run my business?
In most cases the answer is yes. Most cities do require some type of license to operate a business out of your home. You can acquire this license by going to your local city/town hall or county agency. The cost is usually somewhere between $10-$50 depending upon where you live. You may also contact your local chapter of the Small Business Administration for questions or additional information.

Is it legal to work at home?
In most cases it is legal. It depends upon your local zoning ordinance. Before you start your business, you should find out what the zoning laws are in your area.

What does DBA stand for?

The term "DBA" stands for "doing business as" meaning that if checks come to you in any other name than your own, you will need to set up a bank account at your bank with your name DBA "Whatever you decide to name your business." To avoid any problems, you can use, "Your name and Associates," if you choose.

Supplies and other items needed to get started:

Supplies to get started include letterhead, envelopes and business cards. It is important to choose quality stock for your letterhead and business cards since first impressions can last a lifetime.

It is imperative that you open up a separate business checking account at your bank so that you can keep your transactions separate from your personal account. When you purchase things such as letterhead, business cards or office equipment, pay for those items with a check from your business account so that those expenses can be written off at the end of the year.

NOTES

NOTES

NOTES

NOTES

NOTES

Chapter Two

Recruiting 101

Having gone through the basics of being an entrepreneur, let's get down to the specifics of recruiting. What is recruiting anyway? Recruiting is the process of identifying qualified candidates for career opportunities and presenting their backgrounds to client companies, who pay you a fee if and when the candidate is brought on board. For example, if a company has a need for a marketing director and you present a candidate with the appropriate qualifications who gets hired, that company will pay you a placement fee. Sounds simple enough, but how do you identify the companies who are hiring and the people who are interested in new career opportunities? In the pages that follow, you will find the answers to these questions and more about the recruiting industry and operating a home-based recruiting business.

Before we begin explaining techniques that can be used in your recruiting business, we need to put the concept itself into context. There are several reasons that companies pay independent recruiters to help fill their job openings. One of the main reasons is that companies sometimes cannot find the individuals they are seeking by using their own methods such as employee referrals or running newspaper ads. As a matter of fact, running ads in the newspaper is one of the most ineffective ways for companies to find qualified candidates because it limits the audience to only those who are reading the employment ads each week. Companies realize this, and as a result, they sometimes rely on recruiters to bring them qualified candidates that could not be found through their own methods of recruiting. Similar to the way a real estate broker brings buyers and sellers together, a recruiter brings qualified candidates together with client companies. The difference is that as a recruiter, it is possible to do all of your work at home by telephone and fax.

Recruiting is not necessarily difficult or complex. However, it does require a solid set of business skills. You need these skills to articulate yourself professionally when you are presenting a career opportunity over the telephone to a candidate. You also need a strong set of customer service skills so that companies will have confidence in your services. Clients will want to know that they can rely on you for good service. Lastly, you must be a self-motivated and ambitious individual to survive in the recruiting industry. These traits will carry you a long way in this business!

A foundation of knowledge about recruiting is not enough. You also need to be thinking about creating an identity for yourself by determining which industry you want to recruit in and what you are going to call yourself. It is very common for individuals in this line of work to call themselves search consultants, contract recruiters or staffing consultants. These terms all mean the same thing and companies as well as candidates will know why you are calling the second they hear your title. As far as industries are concerned, you do not have to be married to any one industry. You can recruit for virtually any industry. However, if you have knowledge of a particular industry, it can only be to your advantage to recruit within that space. Today, there are companies in almost all major industries that pay fees to outside recruiters who fill their openings with qualified candidates. Once you have narrowed down the industries you have decided to work in, go to your local library or bookstore, or check out the Internet to get a list of companies, their contact information and company history. You will quickly learn who the key players are and may now start to develop a strategy of whom you would like to recruit for and from. From this list, you will begin making calls to hiring managers and human resource representatives to start securing job orders.

Once you have identified the industry you have chosen to work in as well as a list of companies to call, you are almost ready to begin making calls and securing information about job openings and available candidates. However, you will first need to develop a script. As recruiters, there are two types of presentations we make over the telephone. We present career opportunities to candidates who are looking to advance their careers and we present candidates' backgrounds to companies who are hiring. Developing an effective presentation that you are comfortable with requires a bit of rehearsal before you get on the telephone to make the actual calls. The following are sample scripts to get you started.

Calling a company

In this conversation, your main goals are an interview for the candidate you are presenting and to learn about any other job openings the company may have and may need assistance with. There are three parts to every marketing call. The first few seconds of your call, you should be introducing yourself and where you are calling from. The next few seconds should be spent informing the person about the services you have to offer. The last few seconds of the call, you should be explaining how and why this company will benefit from your services. Get to the point! This is what your listener's want. Tell them what they need to hear right away while you have their undivided attention.

"Hi Jeff, this is Madelyn. I am a staffing consultant at ABC Recruiting in New York. How are you today?"

"Just fine Madelyn, how can I help you today?"

"Well Jeff, the reason for my call is to introduce a senior marketing professional with 20 years experience. He has expressed interest in working with your company. He currently works for one of your key competitors and was ranked as one of the top three sales and marketing professionals in his current company last year."

"Interesting. Why is he looking for a change?"

"Actually, the division he works in is moving all of their sales and marketing staff to California and he would like to stay in New York. He is particularly interested in your company because of the outstanding reputation you hold."

"What else do you know about this guy?"

"Well, he graduated from Stanford with a Master's in Business Management 10 years ago and has been at his current company since then. He started out as a sales assistant and has been promoted four times in 10 years. He is a very assertive individual. He is extremely well spoken and has an impeccable level of professionalism."

"Where is he on the salary scale?"

"His total package is $100,000 annually. His base salary is $75,000 and he earns approximately $25,000 per year in commission. He also has excellent benefits, a 401K plan and stock options."

"Sounds very similar to what we pay. Do you have his resume?"

"Sure, I'll e-mail it to you. What is your e-mail address?"

"jeff@johndoeassociates.com."

"Great. By the way, if this candidate is someone you decide to proceed with, what type of salary package do you offer?"

"$75,000-$85,000 base salary with a potential bonus of $30,000 per year, which is paid quarterly."

"Thanks Jeff. I'll get this resume over to you right away and follow up with you on Monday of next week. I do operate on a 25 percent contingency fee basis if the candidate gets hired. Are you authorized to sign off on something like this?

"Yes, and 25 percent seems pretty standard these days, so that won't be a problem. Are you going to e-mail a fee agreement with that resume?"

"I'll be happy to do that and again, I will follow up with you on Monday of next week. Will 10 a.m. work for you?"

"Perfect."

"Great, It was nice talking to you Jeff, and I'll talk with you on Monday."

This script was provided as an example. When making your own script, you may choose to ask different questions until you feel comfortable with your presentation.

Other sample questions you could ask when taking job specifications are as follows:

What are the key responsibilities of this position?

What is the title of the open position?

How many years experience are required?

What are the educational requirements?

How many years experience are you looking for?

Who will this person report to and how does it fit into your organization?

What is the breakdown on the compensation package?

How much travel is involved with the position?

Will this person have anyone reporting to him/her?

Which location will this person be based out of?

What skill sets are needed to be successful in this position?

Why is this position open?

What have you already done to try and fill this position?

How long has the position been vacant?

When thinking of questions, imagine you are the candidate. What would you like to know about a new position you were considering?

Calling a candidate

In this conversation, your goal is to test the candidate's interest level in the position. Be very thorough when educating the candidate on the position and try to get a copy of a recent resume.

"Hi Drew, this is Madelyn Johnson, I'm a staffing consultant here in New York. I am calling you regarding a career opportunity with one of the key players in the marketing arena. How are you today?"

"Just fine. What type of position is it and where is it located?"

"It is a senior marketing director position located here in New York City."

"How did you get my name?"

"I got your name out of the American Marketing Association Member Directory."

"Well great! What else can you tell me about the position?"

"This position is based here in New York City and is with a Fortune 500 company. The title of the job is senior marketing director. Responsibilities include management of six sales representatives, sales and marketing fore casting, overseeing the marketing departments budget and handling day-to-day operations. The department consists of 60 people and you would be reporting to the vice president."

"This sounds very interesting. What is the next step in the process?"

"I need a current copy of your resume if you would like to be considered for the position. If you are qualified, I will present it to my client on your behalf. Once they have reviewed your resume, I'll keep you updated on how they would like to proceed."

"I'll get that over to you this afternoon. What is your fax number?

"It is 212-555-1212 and you can fax it to me, Madelyn Johnson. As I said before, I'll review your resume and get back to you. Is this the best number to reach you?"

"Yes it is."

"Great. It was nice talking with you and I'll be in touch with you soon."

When you are new to the business, you may be less selective about the jobs you take on. However, once you're a bit more seasoned, you will realize that you can choose the searches you conduct. You will learn over time how to prioritize your searches. For example, when you are working on a search, you should always evaluate the situation to see if there is a sense of urgency behind filling the position. If the company is in no hurry to fill the position, you should focus your efforts on another search where you will achieve more immediate results. Also, don't ever waste time talking to individuals within a company who are not authorized to make the decisions or allocate money for staffing.

Now that we have a script, the question comes down to whom we are going to call. Refer to an industry directory or company contact list you have generated. If you do not have a contact name, simply start in the Human Resources department, where company hiring usually originates. You can ask for a recruiter or the staffing manager. The other half of the equation on the company side of things is a specific department manager, usually referred to as the "hiring manager" of that department. These individuals have an important say in who gets hired in the department. They work hand in hand with the recruiters or staffing managers to identify qualified candidates who fit their openings.

It is of utmost importance to also understand the hierarchy of people within an organization you are calling. Understanding this structure will assist you in maneuvering your way around a company by telephone and get to specific people that you may need to speak with. Every department has senior employees who are very seasoned, junior employees with little or hardly any experience and a lot of people who fall in between. For example, a marketing department may look something like this: administrative assistant, marketing assistant, marketing representative, marketing specialist, marketing supervisor, marketing manager, director of marketing and vice president of marketing.

You may be asking yourself why you need to know all of this. It is important that you are informed so that when you're calling into these companies, you can use people's titles as a way of identifying the right people to talk to for securing potential candidates or job orders. Knowing how any organization is structured can only help you. You are much more prepared to effectively target the right audience.

Now that you have the ammunition you need to go into these companies, let's get back to what you are going to do once you have contacted the company, they have expressed interest in your candidate and an interview has taken place. After the interview, contact the company and the candidate for feedback. Ask a lot of questions (known as probing) to assess the interest level of both parties involved. Questions you might ask the company include:

How was the interview?

What did you like or dislike about the candidate?

Do you feel that his/her qualifications were in line with your expectations?

In what areas could he/she improve?

Are you prepared to offer this candidate a job?

Questions you might ask a candidate include:

How was the interview?

Who did you meet with?

Do you feel like you are qualified for the position?

What did you like or dislike about the company?

How long did the interview last?

If you were offered this position today, would you accept it?

This process of following up and asking each party questions is known as debriefing and is a very important stage in the process. Take in all of the information you possibly can at this stage so that you have the knowledge to develop a strategy to resolve any issues that may stand in the way of the company hiring this individual.

If your client or your candidate is not interested in moving forward, your next step is to call the other party and make them aware of the decision that has been made. Sharing negative feedback is not the most pleasurable experience, but you will find that both your clients and your candidates will appreciate your honesty.

Once a candidate has interviewed and there is interest from both parties, you can assure yourself that the salary issue will be the next thing to come up. Part of being a solid recruiter is salary negotiating. This is an essential part of closing deals. You need to learn your candidates' salary expectations in the beginning. You also need to be very clear on the range of pay that the company is willing to pay. You are a facilitator. Your job is to inform and consult with both parties on what a reasonable compensation might be under these particular circumstances. The old saying is "Close your candidates low and your companies high," meaning get a verbal commitment from your candidate that they will accept a salary at a certain amount and try to get your client to come up with as high an offer as possible. That way, you will have room to work with during the negotiation process if you need it.

After the salary negotiation stage and if your client is ready to proceed with an offer, you must check the candidate's references. If the client is satisfied with the results of the references, you may extend the offer to the candidate. Once you have received acceptance on an offer, call your client to confirm the candidate's start date. Make sure that this information is communicated clearly to the candidate. Scenarios where a candidate accepts a job and never shows up for work do happen. It's not a bad idea to call the employee during their first week of work as well to congratulate him/her and verify that they have actually started.

At this point, you're probably starting to get the hang of this process and now you're wondering how you get paid. It begins with a standard fee agreement (you will find a sample contingency fee agreement in the forms section of this book). When a company gives you a job order, you should always fax them a fee agreement. This agreement should be signed with an authorized signature and returned before the process goes any further.

There are two types of agreements: contingency and retained. Contingency means that the company will pay you a fee contingent on the fact that they hire a candidate that you have presented. You are *not* paid for submitting candidates who are not hired. However, if they do hire a candidate that you have submitted, you are paid a fee equal to a percentage of that candidate's annual salary. The percentage depends upon what your agreement states. More than likely, you will be starting out working on a contingency basis. If you decide to work on a retained basis, there are some differences. In this case, a company retains you to find a certain type of individual for them. In other words, the company will pay you a set fee up front to go out and find the exact type of person they are seeking. In turn, you would go identify that person. Securing contracts on a retained basis can be extremely complicated if you are just starting out because you have not established credibility for being a solid recruiter. That type of relationship comes over time. Once you have worked with and established rapport with a client or filled several positions for them, you may be able to land a retained search contract.

Let's review some of the information that we have covered by looking at it in short form. The following list is a quick reference tool to the 15 steps of recruiting:

The 15 Steps to Recruiting

1. Take a complete and accurate job order.
2. Develop a recruiting strategy or a plan of action that you intend to follow.
3. Source for candidates (a list of sourcing methods is included in chapter 5).
4. Contact any and all appropriate qualified candidates and run the position by them.
5. Present your best and most qualified candidates to your client.
6. Set up first interview between client and candidate.
7. Follow up with and debrief both client and candidate.
8. Schedule second and third interviews if needed.
9. Do reference checks. (Sample form in chapter 4).
10. Salary negotiations with both parties.
11. Present the final offer to the candidate.
12. Make a follow-up call to make sure the candidate has actually started work.
13. Prepare and send the billing invoice to the client.
14. Send a thank you note to both the client and the candidate.
15. Check in with the client and the candidate after three months of employment.

Let's put everything into proper sequence to help you get started. The first step is to identify the industry you are going to work in and develop a source list that includes company names, phone numbers, contact names, etc. (In chapter five, there is a list of resources to assist you in developing this list.) This list will serve as your road map. Now you will need to develop a script that you plan to use to market your services. Once you have these tools and have rehearsed your script, you are ready to begin making calls. Once you find candidates who are qualified and interested, you may begin setting up interviews. Remember to give your candidate any information you may have that may help them or improve their performance on the interview. Once the interview has taken place, debrief both your client and the candidate. If there is a need for a second or third round of interviews, coordinate those accordingly and be sure to address salary expectations with your candidate. If the company does want to offer your candidate the position, check the candidates' references, handle the salary negotiation process and then proceed with making the offer. Once your offer is accepted, congratulate both parties and call to confirm a start date. Send your invoice out to the client and be sure to follow up after three months of employment. The only thing left to do is wait to collect your hard earned reward!

NOTES

NOTES

NOTES

NOTES

NOTES

Chapter Three

Interviewing

This chapter will be a great reference tool for those of you who have never interviewed anyone before. We will cover what questions you should be asking as well as those you should never ask. We will go over the appropriate questions to ask when screening an applicant as well as the questions to ask when interviewing to determine whether or not this person might be a viable candidate for your position. Let's start with a list of questions that you should never ask. They are as follows:

1. Are you married, widowed, divorced or separated?
2. How old are you-when is your birthday?
3. What is your race?
4. What is your sex?
5. How many children do you have?
6. Are you pregnant?
7. Do you have cancer, AIDS, epilepsy, etc.?
8. Do you have an addiction to drugs or alcohol?
9. Have you ever been arrested?
10. Do you own your home?
11. What is your height/weight?
12. When did you graduate from high school? College?
13. What religion are you? What is the name of your church?

All qualified candidates must be considered for a position regardless of their age, race, religion, handicap or national origin. If any company asks you to screen employees illegally, you should politely inform them that they are violating the law and refuse the job assignment.

The following is a list of legal screening questions you can consider using when talking to a candidate for the first time. The goal here is to make sure both you and the candidate are on the same page. Before you ask these questions, the candidate should have been given a brief job description and a salary range of the position.

1. Based on the overview of the responsibilities and salary range, is this a position you are interested in hearing more about?
2. Does the salary range meet your expectations for this type of position?
3. Can you tell me about your current organization and the position you now hold?
4. How do you feel your past work experiences have prepared you for this position?
5. What do you like/dislike about your current position?
6. What specific traits have contributed to your success as a _____?
7. What part of your job do you consider to be the most important?
8. Can you describe your work style to me? Any adjectives that describe you?
9. What computer skills do you have?
10. Is there anything else you feel I should know about you?

Based on the above questions, you should be able to make a decision as to whether or not it would be in your best interest to proceed any further with a particular candidate. You will sometimes find that after an initial screening, a candidate may not be appropriate for the job you had in mind, but may be perfect for another.

If, after the initial screening, there is mutual interest between you and the candidate, a more thorough interview is necessary. Obviously, the questions you will ask will vary on each interview and what you ask will depend upon the specifications of the job. The following questions are samples that can assist you in the interviewing process.

1. Tell me about the largest work decision you have had to make in your career. How did you come to that decision?
2. Describe a major work problem you have faced and how you dealt with it.
3. Tell me about a work situation in which you have been part of a problem. How did you handle the situation?
4. Would you describe yourself as being more logical or intuitive when solving problems? Why?
5. Have you ever been tempted to break a work policy for a special situation?
6. Have you ever worked in an environment where there were continuous changes in management and policies? How did you react to those changes?
7. Give me a brief summary of any leadership positions you have held in your career.
8. What has been your greatest accomplishment in your career?
9. Where do you feel you have left your largest thumbprint in your career?
10. What kind of preparation did you do for this interview?
11. Why should my client hire you?
12. How do you go about building rapport with clients and colleagues?
13. Describe a situation where you had to support your colleagues or management team even when you disagreed with them.
14. What qualities or skill sets do you feel you possess that would make you successful in this type of role?
15. How long have you been in your current industry?
16. Whom do you report to?

17. Do you have anyone reporting to you?
18. Where did you go to college? Do you have a degree? When did you graduate?
19. Where do you see yourself in three to five years?
20. Where do you see yourself in 10 to 12 years?
21. What would prompt you to look at a new career opportunity?
22. Do you have any accomplishments you are particularly proud of?
23. What is the breakdown on your current complete compensation package?
24. Do you participate in continuing education classes or activities now?
25. What magazines do you read? What was the last book you read?
26. Are you willing to travel? If so, how much?
27. In what areas would you require the support of partners and associates?
28. Do your future goals include becoming an entrepreneur or firm owner?
29. How do you spend your free time?
30. Why are you thinking about changing careers?
31. Describe some of your best client relationships.
32. Do you socialize with any of your clients?
33. What would your colleagues say about you?
34. What would your current manager have to say about you?
35. If we were to offer you a position, when could you start?

When asking candidates questions, keep them talking about themselves. This will provide you with a steady stream of information as well as fill you in on how this person organizes their thoughts and how they articulate this information to you.

Tips for effective interviewing

Be relaxed. The more relaxed you are, the more relaxed the candidate will be. You will find that candidates who are relaxed tend to open up more about themselves.

Be a good listener!

Take extensive notes when interviewing a candidate. Otherwise, you won't remember half of the information you talked about later in the week.

Do not show approval or disapproval of what the candidate is saying. You need this person to tell you the truth, not what they think you want to hear.

Never interrupt a candidate. You will most likely miss out on a piece of valuable information if you interrupt.

Try to avoid any and all interruptions and distractions if at all possible.

In interviewing a candidate, treat the situation as a peer talking to another peer as opposed to a formal interview where you are the interviewing authority. This will help the candidate become more relaxed and warm up to you. Look for consistency in the interview. Always ask about any conflicting or contradictory statements right then and there. Pay attention to your gut reaction to an interview. Has this person been direct with you? Have they been honest with you? All of these points should be taken into consideration. At the close of the interview, you should ask the candidate for at least three to five professional references if the candidate hasn't already provided them. The references need to be relatively current. Going back six to eight years is not going to be particularly useful. Recent and current supervisors and colleagues are your best bet. Please refer to the candidate reference check form in chapter four.

After the interview, always keep candidates informed of their status. As a recruiter, you will earn respect from your clients and candidates if you consistently follow up with everyone and keep all parties abreast of what is happening at each stage in the process.

The following is a list of judgment words, attributes and phrases.

above board	dedicated	rational
achiever	dynamic	reliable
aggressive	extrovert	reputable
ambitious	honest	savvy
articulate	independent	scrupulous
assertive	imaginative	self assured
bubbly	initiates	solid experience
candid	lively	solution seeker
capable	mellow	spontaneous
challenging	motivated	sunny disposition
comprehensive	perceptive	team player
conscientious	polished	tenacious
confident	proficient	well mannered
creative	passive	witty

NOTES

NOTES

NOTES

NOTES

NOTES

Chapter Four

Sample Forms and Letters

This chapter is loaded with useful forms, letters and tools you will use in this business. You have been provided with ready-made forms for recruiting, tracking information and telephone calls, reference checking and more. You can copy them and begin using them right away. However, you must keep in mind that these are sample forms and you may decide to make your own forms or use something different that works best with your individual recruiting style. The information provided in this chapter will give you a head start in the recruiting business.

Marketing/Introduction Letter

John Doe & Associates
555 Any Street
Dedham, Ma 00000

Dear John,

As an introduction to Beachwood Associates, I am enclosing some information about our company and what we have to offer.

Beachwood Associates specializes in providing client companies with top quality professionals on a permanent basis.

Our qualified staff offers a vast knowledge of the market place. I am confident that our services would be a valuable investment toward your continued success. I welcome the opportunity to discuss the advantages of utilizing our firm to assist you with your staffing needs. I look forward to speaking with you soon.

Kind Regards,

Beachwood Associates

NOTE: You will send any promotional material as well as a sample recruiting agreement with this form. Remember to *always* get the recruiting agreement signed before you send any resumes.

Letter To fax to "network" for job orders and resumes

John Doe & Associates
555 Any Street
Dedham, Ma 00000

Dear Mr. Doe,

This letter is in follow-up to our conversation earlier today.

As I explained on the telephone, our recruiting agency is new in the area. Since we are in the same industry, I thought it would be a good idea if we pulled our resources together and networked with one another. I have an extensive resume database. If you have any current job orders, we could split the fee on a 50/50 basis. We also have job orders from numerous companies and I would be pleased to share those with you as well.

Please fax me a copy of your referral agreement so that we can fee-share, or if you prefer, I will fax you a copy of our referral agreement to you. I look forward to working with you!

Kind Regards,

Beachwood Associates

NOTE: Fax or mail this letter to other recruiting firms in your same area of specialty.

Form for your fax cover sheet

Facsimile Cover Sheet

DATE:

PAGES:

TO: FROM:

FAX NUMBER: FAX NUMBER:

COMMENTS/NOTES:

Fee Schedule

January 1, 1999

John Doe, Director of Human Resources
John Doe & Associates
555 Any Street
Dedham, Ma 00000

Dear John,

We appreciate your interest in _____(your company name). You will be pleased to know that our fees are below the industry standard. We keep our fees reasonable because we appreciate your efforts to hire new personnel on the best terms possible. We hope that you will remember us in the future when you have additional staffing needs. Our fees are as follows:

1.) For each hired candidate, _____(company name) will pay _____(your company name) a fee equal to 30% of the candidates first year salary.

2.) All fees shall be payable within 30 days of candidates start date.

Our recruiting agreement is enclosed. Please sign the agreement where indicated and fax it back to _____(your fax number). Upon receiving the agreement we will immediately begin our search. Thank you for your job order and we look forward to assisting you with all of your staffing needs in the future.

Kind Regards,

Beachwood Associates

NOTE: Send this form to new clients. You may charge any percentage you would like. Keep in mind that 30% is the average.

Invoice to send to clients to request payment for services

John Doe and Associates
555 Any Street
Dedham, Ma 00000

INVOICE #100

We have been informed that _____will start working for your organization on the _____day of _____, 19____. Please send a check in the amount of $_____ representing payment in full on the Recruiting Agreement which was signed on _____, 19____. We appreciate your business and look forward to assisting you in all of your future staffing needs. Payment should be made to our address as shown above.

NOW DUE AND PAYABLE FOR PLACEMENT SERVICES:
$_____

NOTE: Mail the invoice the same day that you confirm with the candidate that he/she has accepted an employment offer with the company.

Recruiter's Fee Sharing Agreement

This Recruiter's fee sharing agreement (the "Agreement") is entered into effective this_____ day of _____, 200_ by and between "Recruiter A" and "Recruiter B", whose names and addresses appear below.

Recruiter A and Recruiter B mutually hereby agree as follows:

1. *Undertaking Of Recruiter.* Recruiter A agrees to use its best efforts in an attempt to find either: (a) a suitable CANDIDATE for a JOB ORDER that Recruiter B has, or (b) to find a suitable JOB ORDER for a CANDIDATE that Recruiter B has. The specific JOB ORDER(s) or CANDIDATE(s) will follow by subsequent faxes.

2. *Confidentiality.* Recruiter A and Recruiter B each agree to keep all submissions of JOB ORDERS, resumes or CV's submitted by one to the other confidential and not to use, employ or refer to another the CANDIDATE(s) or JOB ORDER(s) without payment of referral fees as set forth in Paragraph 3., below.

3. *Sharing Of Fee Payments Received.* In the event that Recruiter A submits a CANDIDATE to Recruiter B and that CANDIDATE is hired as a result of a JOB ORDER belonging to Recruiter B, then Recruiter A shall be entitled to a referral fee payable by Recruiter B equal to fifty percent (50%) of the amount received by Recruiter B from the total placement fee as evidenced by a copy of the check received by Recruiter B, which shall accompany payment of the referral fee. In the event that Recruiter B submits a CANDIDATE to Recruiter A and the CANDIDATE is hired as a result of a JOB ORDER belonging to Recruiter A, then Recruiter B shall be entitled to a referral fee payable by Recruiter A equal to fifty percent (50%) of the amount received by Recruiter A from the total placement fee as evidenced by a copy of the check received by Recruiter A, which shall accompany payment of the referral fee. Payment of referral fees under this agreement are due and payable within three (3) business days after receipt of payment(s) is received form the employer who authorized the JOB ORDER.

4. *Other Terms.* Any amendment of this Agreement shall be in writing. In the event that either Recruiter fails to pay the other Recruiter referral fees owed under this Agreement, the prevailing party in any legal action shall be entitled to recover reasonable attorney's fee and court costs in addition to damages. Signatures received by fax shall be deemed as fully valid as if they were original signatures. Fees received on placements may be subject to certain conditions such as completion of a minimum satisfactory work period by the Candidate before the placement fee becomes final and payable.

Agreed the date first above written in the County of _____, State of _____, by and between the following:

_____   _____
"Recruiter A" (signature)   "Recruiter B" (signature)

Print your Name: Print your Name:
Address: Address:
City: City:

State & Zip   State & Zip
Tel. (   )   Tel. (   )
Fax (   )   Fax (   )

NOTE: This is the Fee Sharing Agreement that is to be used when working with another recruiter.

Recruiting Agreement

This Recruiting Agreement (the "Agreement") is made and entered into this _____ day of _____, 19___ by and between _____, DBA _____(your company name), "RECRUITER," whose business address is listed below and "CLIENT," whose name and address appear below. RECRUITER and CLIENT are jointly referred to as the parties.

In consideration of the mutual covenants and agreements hereinafter set forth, the parties do hereby agree as follows:

1.   *Recruiter Responsibilities.* Recruiter shall be responsible to locate, screen and make preliminary reference checks on any and all CANDIDATE(S) according to CLIENT'S requirements. Prospective CANDIDATES suitable for CLIENT'S requirements will be introduced to CLIENT and assistance given to CLIENT and CANDIDATE in the negotiations leading to a mutually satisfactory contract of employment.

2.   *Client's Responsibilities.* Client will process all CANDIDATES in an expeditious, professional manner and keep RECRUITER informed on a current basis of negotiations with CANDIDATES. CLIENT understands that time is of the essence in the setting of an interview date, qualifications review and employment negotiations with CANDIDATES. Final reference checks and any other documentation deemed necessary by the CLIENT shall be obtained at the expense of the CLIENT.

3.   *Payment Fees.* CLIENT shall pay to RECRUITER a fee equal to thirty percent of the candidates first year salary. This is the standard "fee"

for each CANDIDATE hired, retained or employed by CLIENT as an employee, independent contractor or in any other capacity. One hundred percent (100%) of the total Fee is due and payable within thirty (30) days of the date that CANDIDATE first commences work for the CLIENT.

4. *Client Guarantee.* In the event that CANDIDATE fails to meet obligations to CLIENT, through no fault of CLIENT, during the initial period of employment not to exceed ninety (90) days, then CLIENT shall so notify RECRUITER in writing. In the event that the CANDIDATE shall no longer be employed by the CLIENT within thirty (30) days after his/her start date, then RECRUITER shall refund to CLIENT ninety percent (90%) of the fee paid; alternatively, in the event that the CANDIDATE shall no longer be employed by CLIENT within sixty (60) days after his/her start date, then RECRUITER shall refund to CLIENT sixty percent (60%) of the fee paid; alternatively, in the event that the CANDIDATE shall no longer be employed by CLIENT within ninety (90) days of his/her start date, then RECRUITER shall refund to CLIENT thirty percent (30%) of the fee paid. If CANDIDATE has been employed by CLIENT for more than ninety (90) days, no portion of the fee will be refunded.

5. *Expenses Of The Parties.* RECRUITER shall bear its own expenses for locating and recruiting CANDIDATES acceptable to CLIENT. All other expenses shall be borne by CLIENT, including travel and related expenses for CANDIDATE(S) invited by CLIENT to review the facilities and community being considered for prospective employment.

6. *Subsequent Candidate Placement.* CLIENT agrees that should it, or a third party introduced to the CANDIDATE by the CLIENT, enter into a contract of employment (either verbal or written) within a period of two (2) years after first having been introduced to the CANDIDATE by

the RECRUITER, then the RECRUITER shall be deemed to have performed its obligation hereunder and the full fee shall be payable to RECRUITER by CLIENT as set forth in Paragraph 3., above.

7. *Standard Provisions.* 7.1 The parties agree to conduct their activities hereunder in accordance with applicable professional ethical standards and with all applicable federal, state and local laws, including, but not limited to, equal employment opportunity laws and regulations. 7.2 This Agreement contains the entire understanding and agreement between the parties with respect to the matters referred to herein. No other representations, covenants, undertakings, warranties, guarantees or other prior or contemporaneous agreements, oral or written, respecting such matters, which are not specifically incorporated herein, shall be deemed in any way to exist or bind any of the parties.

This Agreement, and the covenants and conditions contained herein, shall apply to, be binding upon, and inure to the administrators, heirs, executors, legal representatives, assignees, successors, agents and assigns of the parties. 7.4 This Agreement shall be governed by the laws of the State of _____ and the parties agree to submit solely to the jurisdiction of the courts of the State of _____, County of _____, or the Federal District Court for said district, in the event of any dispute or suit regarding, concerning, or arising out of this Agreement or its performance. In the event of any litigation {trial or appellate} arising out of the Agreement, the prevailing party shall be entitled to reasonable attorney's fees in addition to costs of suit and any damages that may be awarded. 7.5 In the event that any portion of the Fee due and payable to Recruiter is not timely paid it shall be deemed to be the principal and bear interest at one and one-half percent (1.5%) per month until both principal and interest are paid in full. 7.6 This Agreement may be executed in multiple counterparts, each of which shall be deemed an original

Agreement, and all of which shall constitute one Agreement. 7.7 This Agreement, and Candidate information, may be accepted, executed and delivered by fax transmission and it shall be deemed to have the same validity as if accepted, executed and delivered by post or in person. 7.8 This Agreement shall not be amended or modified except by written agreement executed by both of the parties.

In witness whereof, the parties have caused this agreement to be executed by their authorized representative on the day and date first above written,

BY:_____   BY:_____

"Recruiter," Dated: "Client," Dated:

Company Name: Company Name:

Agent's Name: Agent's Name:

Address: Address:

City: City:

State: Zip: State: Zip:

Tel. (   )   Tel. (   )

Fax (   )   Fax (   )

NOTE: This is the agreement to be sent to all potential clients.

Candidate Reference Check Form

Applicant: **Date:**

Contact: **Title:**

Company: **Phone:**

1. What is/was your relationship to the candidate?
2. What are/were his/her responsibilities?
3. What are his/her strengths?
4. On a scale of 1-10 (10=superior & 1=poor), how would you rank him/her in the following areas?

_____ Decision-making skills   _____ Initiative

_____ Client rapport   _____ Attitude

_____ Communication skills   _____ Organizational skills

_____ Punctuality   _____ Flexibility

_____ Computer skills   _____ Commitment to job

_____ Ability to handle pressure   _____ Quality of work

5. Are there any areas where he/she could use improvement?
6. Do you have any other information that would help me develop a more complete picture of him/her?
7. If you had an open position, would you rehire him/her?
8. How would you rank this individual against others you have known in the same capacity?

Weekly Plan of Action Page

Date: _____   **Day of Week:** _____

Make several copies of this page and place them in a three-ring binder to help maintain organization. This page will help you manage your time more efficiently. Note any high priority calls or things to get done for the week here.

Who was called (name/address)	Phone # (& area code)	Activity
1.		
2.		
3.		
4.		
5.		
6.		
7.		
8.		
9.		
10.		

Placement Checklist

CLIENT:

PHONE #:

ADDRESS:

JOB TITLE:

SIGNED CONTRACT: Y   N   DATE:

FEE: DATE BILLED:

AMOUNT DUE:

SPECIAL NOTES:

CONGRATULATIONS LETTER SENT TO CANDIDATE: Y   N

DATE SENT:

THANK YOU LETTER SENT TO CLIENT: Y   N

DATE SENT:

THANK YOU LETTER SENT TO CANDIDATE: Y   N

DATE SENT:

REFERRALS: PHONE #
1.   1.
2.   2.
3.   3.
4.   4.
5.   5.

Daily Activity List/Call Sheet

Date	Activity*	Notes/Comments
1.		
2.		
3.		
4.		
5.		
6.		
7.		
8.		
9.		
10.		

*Keep track of types of calls with the following key:
RC=Recruiting call to recruit new candidate
MC=Marketing your services to get new business
FU=Following up with a client or candidate
RF=Calling a referral
RC=Calling to do a reference check

"Thank you for the referral" letter

John Doe
John Doe and Associates
555 Any Street
Dedham, MA 00000

Dear John:

There is no greater compliment our company could receive than a valued client, like you, referring us to a colleague. You made our day when _____ called to give us a new job order.

We are honored to have you as clients and greatly appreciate your continued support of our firm.

Kind Regards,

Beachwood Associates

NOTE: Always send a thank you note to any client or candidate who gives you a referral.

Thank you for the candidate reference

Mr. John Doe, Director
John Doe & Associates
555 Any Street
Dedham, MA 00000

Dear John:

Thank you for taking the time to give a complimentary reference on behalf
of _____(candidate's name). It is not often that busy managers
take time out to recognize the good work of one of their employees.

I am enclosing a business card in the event that you have any additional
comments or questions.

Sincerely,

Beachwood Associates

NOTE: Use this letter to acquire additional leads.

Thank you letter/Securing job order

John Doe, Manager
John Doe & Associates
555 Any Street
Dedham, MA 00000

Dear John:

Thank you for speaking with me today to discuss your recent job order. The principle benefit of our conversation is that now I have a broader knowledge of your company culture, standards and skills requirements. We appreciate your confidence in us and we thank you for providing our firm with the opportunity to prove that we can, and should, be entrusted with your business. _____ (Clients name) I look forward to building a solid business relationship with you and your organization!

Sincerely,

Beachwood Associates

NOTE: Send this form to the client after taking a new job order.

Congratulations letter to candidate

John Doe
555 Any Street
Dedham, MA 00000

Dear John:

Congratulations on your new position at _____ (Company name) We are happy that we could assist you in your career search. Please contact us if you have any questions or concerns in the future.

Best wishes for continuing success in your career!

Kind Regards,

Beachwood Associates

NOTE: Always send a congratulatory letter to candidates and touch base with them from time to time so that they will refer you to others. Also, they may have a need for your services somewhere down the line and you don't want them to forget about you.

Sample job order form

Date:

Source: Ad in Paper   Candidate lead   Event   Client referral
        Placed lead   Marketing call   Call-in   Direct mail

Job Title:
Salary minimum: $ Maximum: $
Comment:

Company:
Address:

Phone: Fax:
Contact: Title: Extension:
E-mail:

Candidate will report to: Title:
Location of job:
Education required:

Required Skills:

Responsibilities:

Comments:

Fee:

Additional Notes:

Sample Interview Worksheet

Date: ID #

Candidate:

Home Phone: Work Phone:

Candidates PIK Rating:

Current or last company:

Title: Reported to:

Accomplishments:

Salary: $

Reason for leaving:

Notes:

Location preference: Salary desired: $

Industry:

Computer skills:

Current or last company:

Title: Reported to:

Accomplishments:

Salary: $

Reason for leaving:

Notes:

Location preference: **Salary desired: $**
Industry:
Computer skills:

Other agencies representing you:

Additional Notes:

Sample phone screen form

Date: Candidate:

Home Phone: Work Phone:

1. How did you hear about us?

2. Where do you live and is this the base location for your search?

3. Who is your current employer and how long have you been there?

4. Why are you looking & how long have you been looking for a new job?

5. What is your current compensation & how is it structured?

6. What are your computer skills?

7. What is your educational background and are you degreed?

8. Do any other agencies represent you?

9. Have you interviewed anywhere yet?

10. What are your career goals & how are you planning to reach them?

11. What components in your next job would make it the "ideal" position?

Acknowledgement of resume

January 1, 1999

Dear Applicant,

Please be advised that we have received your resume and would like to thank you for your interest. Your resume is being evaluated and we are comparing your qualifications with our current needs. If there is a potential job match, we will contact you to arrange for an interview. Otherwise, we will certainly keep your resume on file in the event that another appropriate position becomes available. Once again, thank you for your interest!

Sincerely,

Beachwood Associates

NOTE: Send this letter in response to any resumes that are received, but fit no current positions that you are recruiting for.

"Thank you for doing business with us" letter

January 1, 1999

John Doe
John Doe & Associates
555 Any Street
Dedham, MA 00000

Dear John:

Thank you for having confidence in_____(your company name). As a professional, I understand that first impressions are everlasting, and I appreciate the opportunity to work with your company.

We hope we have met your standards of excellence. John, thanks again for calling upon our firm. I know you had several choices and it means a great deal to me that you chose _____. (your company name)

Kind Regards,

Beachwood Associates

NOTE: Never forget to thank your clients for doing business with you.

Staffing Confirmation Invoice Letter

January 1, 1999

Mr. John Doe
John Doe & Associates
555 Any Street
Dedham, MA 00000

Dear John:

Thank you for allowing_____(your company name) to assist you with your staffing needs. We have agreed to provide_____(client name) with_____(candidate's name), a_____(candidates title), under the following conditions:

Position Title:
Salary:
Fee:

Thank you for having the confidence in our company to choose us as a reliable source for your staffing needs. We are hopeful that you will continue to allow us to assist you with any needs in the future. As always, we encourage any suggestions that you may have.

Sincerely,

Beachwood Associates

NOTE: After filling a position, send this letter along with the invoice to the client.

NOTES

NOTES

NOTES

NOTES

NOTES

Chapter Five

Resources

This chapter has information and resources to assist in your day-to-day operations. At the time this book was published, this information was accurate.

Recruiting Software Products

After you have some recruiting experience under your belt, you may choose to purchase recruiting software to help you maintain your database of candidates and clients as well as assist you in your searches. The following software and automation products are just a few that are available to you.

SOFTWARE NAME	SOLD BY	TELEPHONE NUMBER
Adapt	Bond Associates	804-266-3300
Information Tracking System	Fleetware Systems Inc.	303-530-0598
PC Hunter	Micro J Systems Inc.	800-995-HUNT
Forage Resume	Advanced Information Mgmt.	972-618-4743
SmartSearch II	Advanced Personnel Systems	800-875-0588

SOFTWARE NAME	SOLD BY	TELEPHONE NUMBER
EZaccess	Personic Software Inc.	800-342-2222
WinSearch	Relational Systems Inc.	800-346-7156
Gopher for Windows	Kenneth Peck Associates	970-349-0364
HireTrack	SIMPATIX	877-467-2849
Alexus	Networker	888-345-5345
SimpleSearch	SimpleSoft Inc.	503-620-0636
Safari Head Hunting System	Safari Software Products	920-485-4100
Various Products	Sourcer Products	360-737-9678

Recruiting Networks

The following list is a group of recruiting networks. Depending upon which industry you choose to recruit for, there may be other organizations that cater to that specific industry.

National Personnel Associates	616-455-6555
Recruiters Online Network Inc.	888-810-0110
National Association of Physician Recruiters	800-726-5613
Top Echelon Inc.	330-455-1433
Insurance National Search Inc.	281-497-5840
National Association of Legal Search Consultants	407-774-7880
Alliance of Medical Recruiters	417-866-1898
Data Processing Independent Consultants Exchange	515-280-1144
First Interview Network	www.firstinterview.net

Recruiting Publications

To support the needs of the recruiting industry, a wide selection of publications are at your fingertips. There are numerous publications out there. The following list is just the beginning!

Publication Name	Phone Number	Website Address
Recruiter's OnLine Magazine	888-810-0110	www.recruitersonline.com
Networking News for Recruiters	330-455-1433	www.topechelon.com
E-cruitingbusiness	650-948-9303	www.ecruitingbusiness.com
Fordyce Letter	314-965-3883	www.ipa.com/fordyce/index.html
Executive Recruiter News	800-531-1026	www.kennedyinfo.com
Employment Marketplace	314-569-3095	www.eminfo.com
SI Review	650-948-9303	www.sireport.com
Electronic Recruiting News	800-358-2278	www.interbiznet.com
Executive Search Research Directory	850-235-3733	N/A
Recruiters Online Magazine	888-810-0110	www.recruitersonline.com
Staffing Industry Report	650-948-9303	www.sireport.com

Sites for finding contacts

www.555-1212.com

www.four11.com

www.whowhere.com

www.switchboard.com

Helpful career-related websites

www.1800network.com	1 800 network
www.4work.com	4 Work
www.ozjobs.com	ACO Online
www.adsearch.com	Ad Search
www.adamsjobbank.com	Adams Job Bank
www.americasemployers.com	America's Employers
www.careeramerica.com	Career America
www.careercast.com	Career Cast
www.careercity.com/job/srch/	Career City
www.careerexchange.com	Career Exchange
www.careerexposure.con	Career Exposure
www.careermag.com	Career Magazine
www.careermosaic.com	Career Mosaic
www.careersite.com	Career Site
www.careersurf.com	Career Surf

www.dice.com	Dice
www.dmworld.com	Direct Working World
www.joboptions.com	Espan
www.futureaccess.com	Future Access
www.globaljobnet.com	Global Job Net
www.headhunter.net	Headhunter.net
www.hotjobs.com	Hot Jobs
www.idealjobs.com	Ideal Jobs
www.intellimatch.com	Intellimatch
www.espan.com	Interactive Employment Network
www.jobfront.com	Job Front
www.jobhunting.com	Job Hunting
www.jobsontheweb.com	Jobs on the Web
www.jobtailor.com	Job Tailor
www.monster.com	Monster Board
www.netjobs.com	Net Jobs

www.net-temps.com	Net-Temps
www.passportaccess.com	Passport Access
www.ipa.com	Recruiters Online Network
www.resumeexpress.com	Resume Express Database
www.selectjobs.com	Selectjobs
www.techies.com	Techies
www.batnet.com	Technology Registry
www.computerregister.com	The Computer Register
www.tripod.com	Tripod
www.vault.com	The Vault
www.yahoo.com	Yahoo

Professional Trade Associations

American Association of Home Based Businesses	1-800-447-9710
Society of Human Resources Management	1-800-283-7476
Association of Executive Search Consultants	212-398-9556
National Association for the Self-Employed	1-800-232-6273
Top Echelon Network	330-455-1433
Association of Executive Search Consultants	212-398-9560

National Association of Executive Recruiters   312-701-0744
National Technical Services Association   703-684-4722

Seminars and Courses

AIRS-   www.airsdirectory.com
Teach Internet recruiting strategies
Rise-   www.riseway.com
Provide Internet recruiting seminars

Helpful websites for individuals who work from home

www.gohome.com
Provides numerous articles about working from home

www.nase.org
The website of the National Association for the Self-Employed

www.ushomebusiness.com
Information and resources for home-based businesses

www.ftc.gov/bcp/conline/pubs/invest/homewrk.htm
Information from the Federal Trade Commission about work at home schemes

www.asbaonline.org
The American Small Business Association website

www.morebusiness.com
An online business resource center

www.irs.ustreas.gov/
The official IRS website can answer all of your tax questions

www.hbiweb.com
The Home Business Institute website offers various services and benefits for members

www.hoaa.com
The Home Office Association of America serves home-based and small business professionals

www.nationalbusiness.org
Provides many small business resources

www.nsbu.org
National Small Business United is an organization dedicated to looking out for small business owners

www.sbaer.uca.edu/
The Small Business Advancement National Center provides assistance to small businesses through many electronic resources

www.backup.com
This site offers a backup method to protect your computer files automatically, daily

www.isbc.com
Provides extensive databases on small businesses

www.wilsonweb.com/webmarket/
Effective web marketing ideas and resources for small businesses

www.webcom.com/seaquest/sbrc/
The Small Business Resource Center provides useful information for entrepreneurs and small businesses

www.sb2000.com
The website for the weekly television program that tells the stories of successful entrepreneurs

www.bizmove.com
A comprehensive free resource of small business information

www.sbnpub.com
Small Business News-a small business magazine

www.entamerica.com
Entrepreneurial America provides products and information to support start-up and existing small businesses

www.score.org
Non-profit organization offering small business resources and free counseling services

Meta Search Engines

If you aren't familiar with search engines, you may want to go to http://searchenginewatch.internet.com/ before you begin. This site will provide you with everything you will ever need to know about search engines, including how to utilize them properly. The following is a list of sites that send "spiders" into many different search engines or directories simultaneously to provide you with the information you are seeking.

Dogpile	www.dogpile.com
Ask Jeeves	www.askjeeves.com
Thunderstone	www.thunderstone.com
Oneseek	www.oneseek.com
Cyber411	www.cyber411.com
Starting Point	www.stpt.com
Mamma	www.mamma.com
MetaCrawler	www.metacrawler.com
All 4 One	www.all4one.com
SavvySearch	www.savvysearch.com
Debriefing	www.debriefing.com
The Big Hub	www.thebighub.com
Inference Find	www.infind.com
ProFusion	www.profusion.com

Search Engines

When using search engines to perform a search, keep the following in mind:

Queries
What key words best describe the overall document or subject I am searching for?

Classification
How would the information or document I am searching for be categorized?

Key Points/Subject
What key points are emphasized in the document or information I am seeking? What are the main conclusions of this information?

Mining the Internet for Candidates

Flip searching is one method recruiters use to search the Internet for candidate resumes. Some people view flip searching in a negative light, whereby others see it as an incredible method used for mining the Internet for potential candidates.

This specific type of search locates people who are linked to any given site. This type of search can be performed for any type of industry or company. For instance, if you were searching for engineers who work for a company called ABC, you would first go to the search engine of your choice. You would then enter the following: "link: ABC.com" Your results are going to be sites that are linked to ABC.com. Now, begin searching through your results to find resumes!

Company Databases & Directories

Business USA   1-800-555-5211
This CD-ROM is a very extensive compilation of information. It includes information on more than 10 million U.S. companies. Each company profile includes contact name and titles, industry, company size and whether or not the company is public or private.

American Big Business Directory   1-800-555-5211
This CD-ROM profiles over 150,000 companies and includes such information as company type, products, industry and sales information. This CD also includes contact names for each organization.

Career Search-Integrated Resource System   617-449-0312
Career Search is a database containing over 700,000 company profiles and contact information. This product is updated monthly.

Hoover's Handbook-CD-ROM version   512-454-7778
This CD-ROM provides in-depth information and profiles on more than 2,500 companies and 200 different industries. This CD-ROM is updated quarterly.

Duns Million Dollar Disc Plus   1-800-526-0651
This CD-ROM by Dun & Bradstreet compiles the information from over 400,000 companies. It includes number of employees, annual sales, biographical data of top executives and more.

Corp Tech Directory   1-800-333-8036
This CD-ROM is updated on a quarterly basis and includes data on over 45,000 technology companies. It also lists the name and titles of thousands of executives.

Companies International   1-800-877-GALE
This database contains information on more than 300,000 companies. It also contains contact names, number of employees and industry information.

Harris Complete   1-800-888-5900
This directory of manufacturers is produced by Harris InfoSource. It includes profiles and contact information of over 300,000 companies. It also includes names and titles of over 600,000 executives.

Standard & Poor's Register   1-800-221-5277
This CD-ROM is a database that includes information on over 55,000 companies. It includes contact information, names and titles of executives, and more. This directory is updated quarterly.

Business Periodical Databases

Business Dateline Ondisc   1-800-521-0600
This database is filled with business articles from more than 450 publications. The information you might find in this publication could be anything regarding the economic outlook for a particular area, growth prospects for a company or even which companies are expanding or hiring. This database is updated monthly.

ABI/Inform   1-800-521-0600
This CD-ROM contains articles from over 1,000 business periodicals and trade publications. You can find a plethora of information about hundreds of different industries. This database also includes information regarding industry trends, business products, services and more. It is updated monthly.

Business and Company Profile   1-800-419-0313
This database contains directory information on over 180,000 companies, public and private. It also includes data on business topics such as marketing and advertising, mergers and acquisitions, business law and international business.

Sourcing for Candidates

There are numerous ways to develop names of candidates. This process of identifying specific prospects is often referred to as sourcing. The following is a list of potential places for you to start.

Internet—The World Wide Web is not only for the government and large corporations anymore. It can be an extremely effective tool in locating candidates when used properly. There are hundreds of sites where you can actually view resumes as well as post jobs. Some of them are free and others charge a nominal fee.

Job Fairs—Job Fairs usually consist of a consortium of companies. These events are advertised on the radio and television a lot of times. Therefore, you're likely to get the same kind of individuals you would by advertising in the newspaper.

Direct Sourcing—With this method, you are simply calling a competitor of the company you are recruiting for and asking who is in charge of a specific department. (Known as a "ruse" call) Obviously, you are seeking individuals with similar titles and qualifications as the position you are recruiting for. Once you have a name, call that person to screen and possibly recruit him/her.

Networking—There are a number of organizations out there for recruiters to be a part of. Being a member of any networking group or organization can only help you. The recruiting business is all about "who you know" in many cases, and networking functions will allow you to obtain new contacts.

Colleges—This is a great place to find recent college graduates or alumni. Most colleges have a career center or placement office. The individuals in these offices will be more than happy to work with you.

Referrals—This is probably the best source of all. Word of mouth is the best advertisement in the recruiting business. Referrals can come from colleagues, friends, clients, candidates, or anyone else you know. Ask for referrals and you will get them!

Trade Publications and Journals—If you are seeking candidates in a specific field or industry, you may want to try looking in a journal published specifically for that field. For example, if you are seeking medical professionals, you may want to look through a JAMA (Journal of the American Medical Association) publication for leads or ideas.

Advertising—This method of sourcing is not something you want to rely on. Advertising tends to work better for very general positions, not for specialized positions. Newspaper ads usually produce a number of unqualified applicants and can be very expensive. Therefore, it is probably a better idea to try other methods first.

Associations—If you belong to any associations, you may want to take advantage of who you know. This type of lead can be great for generating referrals.

Additional Resources

Demographics Information

Census Catalog and Guide
202-512-1800
$21.00 Annually

Statistical Abstract of the United States
202-512-1800
$38.00 Annually

Periodicals

Inc.
Small Business Magazine
$19.00 Annually

In Business
Small Business Magazine/bi-monthly
$29.00 Annually

Online Books

Amazon
www.amazon.com

Powell's Bookstore
www.powells.com

Barnes and Noble
www.bn.com

Borders
www.borders.com

Waldenbooks
www.waldenbooks.com

Crown Books
www.crownbooks.com

NOTES

NOTES

NOTES

NOTES

NOTES

Chapter Six

Recruiting Overview

Every successful business must be built on a solid foundation. The information in this chapter is an overview of the main principles we have covered thus far and should be considered the cornerstones of the recruiting business.

Distinguish Yourself From Other Recruiters!

Companies receive numerous calls each day from recruiters soliciting their business. Therefore, you need to distinguish yourself from the rest. Go the extra mile and give your clients value-added services. Provide them with prepared candidates, set up the interviews between the company and candidate, do reference checks on all of your candidates, etc. In other words, make a difference!

Quality Over Quantity!

Your reputation as a recruiter will only be as good as the quality of the resumes you send your clients. Do not "throw paper" at your clients. If your clients had time to sift through numerous resumes looking for qualified candidates, they probably would not have hired you in the first place!

Confidentiality Is Crucial!

You must respect the confidentiality rights of others at all times in this business. Candidates who are seeking new career opportunities typically do not want their existing employers to know about it. You also have an obligation not to divulge certain information that your client may want to keep confidential.

Ask Real Qualifying Questions!

A good recruiter recognizes all of the variables involved when people contemplate changing jobs. Asking real qualifying questions will address issues that can give you insight on what motivates s candidate's behavior when it comes to making a job change. Having this insight is key when evaluating whether or not you are working with individuals who are truly seeking a career change. Asking qualifying questions allows you to know whether or not the candidate is serious or not. A qualifying question would be something such as:

When do you plan on resigning?

or

What start date would you be looking at?

Answers to these types of questions will help you determine if a candidate is sincere about an opportunity you have presented to them.

Ask Solid Closing Questions!

Solid closing questions stimulate commitment to a particular action. Here is an example. You ask a candidate what their current compensation is and they tell you "mid-70s." Has the candidate clearly answered your question? No, they have given you a ballpark figure. The closing question *should* be, "Your salary is in the mid-60s? Therefore, if I tell my client you're making 63,000, would that be accurate?" Giving a number at the bottom of the range they give you is a great way to find out what their actual salary is.

Time Kills All Deals!

Simply put, the longer a candidate has to wait and wonder whether or not the company you submitted his/her resume is interested or not, the closer they get to changing their minds about switching jobs. People sometimes get offended when a company appears indifferent about their resume being submitted. This can turn into a huge issue when your client procrastinates and does not make prompt decisions. You risk losing candidates that you worked very hard to find in the first place. In the interim, a quick call to your candidates will keep good deals from turning into sour ones, even when your client is stuck in first gear.

Be More Than a Recruiter!

This is the most important part of the game. Go the extra mile. Consult with your clients and your candidates. Be someone who influences a companies actions and results in solid, qualified people getting hired. Bring solutions to your clients and assist them all the way through the hiring process. If a hiring manager is indecisive about bringing a particular candidate in for an interview, you should consult with them on the benefits of meeting this person to learn more about them. The bottom line is usually the chemistry between the candidate and the hiring manager. The only way to know if that chemistry is there is to consult with both parties ahead of time. Influence the actions of your clients and candidates by selling them the benefits of each particular action. It is your ability to consult and influence other's actions that will ultimately put you on the road to success.

NOTES

NOTES

NOTES

NOTES

NOTES

Chapter Seven

Glossary of Recruiting Terms

Base Salary—A Guaranteed income that an employee receives when working for a company. Base salary usually makes up the majority of an employee's total compensation package.

Candidate—The individual who has been recruited to pursue a career opportunity.

Client—The company who has hired you to fill a position for them.

Commission—An incentive-based portion of a candidate's total compensation package. Unlike a base salary, commissions are based on performance-based incentives.

Confidentiality—An unwritten rule that applies to all industries that recruiters will keep confidential all of the information that a candidate or company provides them unless otherwise agreed upon.

Contingency Fee Agreement—An agreement between a company and a recruiter that the recruiter will be paid an agreed amount by the company in the event that they hire a candidate presented by the recruiter. In other words, the recruiter's fee is contingent upon one of their candidates being hired by their client.

Counteroffer—When a company learns that a valuable employee is resigning, they will sometimes present a "counteroffer" to that individual to keep them from leaving the company.

Debriefing—After an interview, the conversation between a recruiter and a candidate/company, to educate each party and find out how each would like to proceed.

Hiring Manager—The individual working in a specific department who is sometimes responsible for the hiring.

Human Resources—The main department in a company responsible for staffing and recruitment of new employees.

Industry Directory—Directory of names and phone numbers of companies in a particular industry.

Interview—Meeting between a candidate and company to discuss a job opportunity and learn about one another.

Job Offer—A formal offer of employment extended by a company to a candidate.

Job Order—The specifications of a position that are used to conduct an employee search.

Job Requirements—The skill sets required to be considered "qualified" for a job.

Job Responsibilities—A list of what a job entails on a daily basis.

Job Specifications—The responsibilities and requirements of a particular job.

Name Development—The process of qualifying and developing a candidate for a specific career opportunity.

Name Generation—The process of contacting companies to generate names of individuals whom you can call at a later date to recruit.

Outplacement Firm—An organization that assists individuals in finding new employment once they have lost their job. These firms have information on numerous individuals who have lost their jobs due to company downsizing.

Phone Interview—A conversation by telephone with a candidate to get a feel for their background and personality. This is an excellent opportunity for both parties to evaluate each other.

Placement Fee—A fee paid to a recruiter who has been hired under an agreement. The amount of the fee is calculated or based upon a percentage of the hired candidate's annual salary.

Preparing candidates—Speaking with candidates before an interview to consult with them on the job, responsibilities, etc.

Qualifying—The process of asking numerous questions to determine how qualified an individual is for a position.

Recruiter—An individual who identifies qualified candidates and presents them for potential career opportunities.

Reference Check—A process, authorized by the candidate, of contacting their references to verify that they are indeed qualified.

Relocation Assistance—Financial assistance sometimes offered by a company to help relocate a new employee to the city where their new job is based.

Resignation—When an employee gives formal notice that he/she will be resigning from their current position.

Resume—A chronological description of an individual's professional background. A resume is sometimes also referred to as a "c.v. or curriculum vitae."

Retainer—A fee paid up-front by a company to a recruiter to conduct an employee search.

Salary Expectations—The amount of money a candidate expects to make annually if he/she accepts a position with a company.

Salary Range—The range of salaries that a company expects to pay a qualified candidate who accepts a position.

Sourcing—The process of generating names of potential candidates for opportunities.

Split Fee Agreement—An agreement between two recruiters to split an earned fee if one recruiter's candidate gets hired for the other recruiter's job opening.

Staffing Consultant—A recruiter who consults with candidates and clients on different methods of hiring qualified people for their openings.

Start Date—The date a candidate will commence work on.

Target Market—A group of companies that employ people whom you plan to recruit to fill your job orders.

Value-Added Services—Every action you might take to go the extra mile for your clients. These may include but are not limited to interview coordination, debriefing sessions and reference checks.

NOTES

NOTES

NOTES

NOTES

NOTES

Business Strategies Plan & Outline

Introduction:

I.

      A.

      B.

      C.

II.

      A.

      B.

      C.

III.

      A.

      B.

      C.

IV.

    A.

    B.

    C.

V.

    A.

    B.

    C.

Conclusion:

About the Author

In this publication, Charrissa Cawley shares the recruiting resources and knowledge that have shaped her career as an entrepreneur, recruiter, manager and trainer.

Based on years of hands on experience, Charrissa's innovative ideas and recruiting methods have helped produce great results and performance improvements in new recruiters. She is the founder of Beachwood Associates, a recruitment research firm dedicated to the development of the research process within the recruiting industry.

In addition to starting and managing her own successful business, she has worked with growing corporations and retained search firms across the nation as a recruiter and consultant. Charrissa resides in San Diego, California, with her husband Jeff and daughter Madison.